D1247004

A KID'S LIFE DURING

THE AMERICAN CIVIL WAR

SARAH MACHAJEWSKI

PowerKiDS press.

New York

Published in 2015 by The Rosen Publishing Group, Inc.
29 East 21st Street, New York, NY 10010

First Edition

Editor: Sarah Machajewski
Book Design: Michael J. Flynn

Photo Credits: Cover SuperStock/Getty Images; cover, pp. 1, 3, 4, 6, 8–14, 16–20, 22–24 (background texture) Ozerina Anna/Shutterstock.com; pp. 3, 4, 6, 8–14, 16–20, 22–24 (paper) Paladin12/Shutterstock.com; pp. 5, 8, 9, 13, 15 courtesy of the Library of Congress; p. 7 Colin Bootman/The Bridgeman Art Library/Getty Images; p. 11 egd/Shutterstock.com; p. 12 Jon Bilous/Shutterstock.com; p. 17 Transcendental Graphics/Archive Photos/Getty Images; p. 18 Christian Draghici/Shutterstock.com; p. 19 Lindy Powers/Photolibrary/Getty Images; p. 21 Hulton Archive/Getty Images; p. 22 C. Kurt Holter/Shutterstock.com.

Library of Congress Cataloging-in-Publication Data

Machajewski, Sarah.
 A kid's life during the American Civil War / Sarah Machajewski.
     pages cm. — (How kids lived)
 Includes index.
 ISBN 978-1-4994-0005-2 (pbk.)
 ISBN 978-1-4994-0007-6 (6 pack)
 ISBN 978-1-4994-0004-5 (library binding)
 1. United States—History—Civil War, 1861-1865—Children—Juvenile literature. 2. Children and war—United States—History—19th century—Juvenile literature. I. Title.
 E468.9.M124 2015
 973.7'1—dc23
                                          2014024185

Manufactured in the United States of America

CPSIA Compliance Information: Batch #CW15PK: For Further Information contact Rosen Publishing, New York, New York at 1-800-237-9932

CONTENTS

A NATION DIVIDED

The American Civil war took place from April 1861 to April 1865. A civil war is when groups of people in the same country fight each other. During the American Civil War, people from the Northern states fought people from the Southern states.

Why did they fight? Leaders from the North and South had different ideas about how to run the country. Their ideas were so different that the Southern states decided to break away from the Northern states. They wanted to be their own country. The South became the **Confederacy**, and the North became the **Union**.

The American Civil War lasted four years, which was longer than anyone expected.

LIFE DOWN SOUTH

The North and South had different points of view because life was very different in the two places. Many Southerners had huge farms, called **plantations**. They grew crops such as cotton, rice, and tobacco.

Taking care of plantations was a lot of work. Many plantation owners had black **slaves** who were forced to work without pay. Slaves were property, which meant their masters "owned" them. If the slaves had children, the children became the property of the slave master, too. Slavery allowed plantation owners to make a lot of money since they didn't have to pay their workers.

White and black children's lives were very different during the Civil War **era**.

SLAVE CHILDREN

Half of all slaves in the American South were under the age of 16. Most slave children began working in the fields by the time they were 8 years old.

LIFE UP NORTH

Life in the North was very different. Most people lived in cities. Instead of plantations, the North had factories. The machines worked faster than people did. Factories showed that slave labor wasn't necessary. Additionally, many Northerners thought slavery was wrong. Most blacks who lived in the North were free.

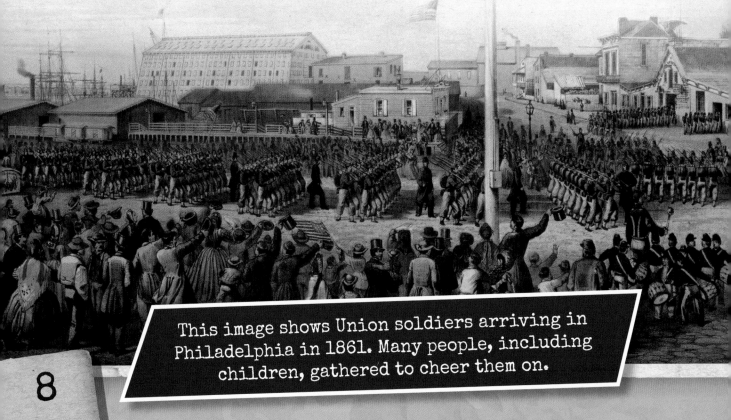

This image shows Union soldiers arriving in Philadelphia in 1861. Many people, including children, gathered to cheer them on.

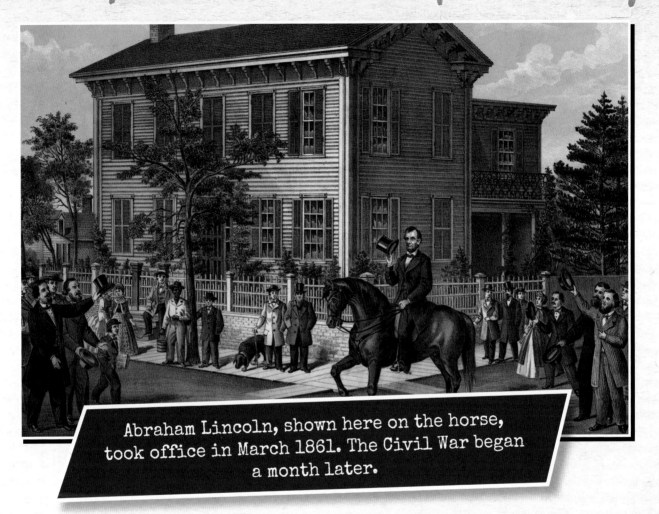

Abraham Lincoln, shown here on the horse, took office in March 1861. The Civil War began a month later.

Southern states didn't want to be forced to give up slavery. They felt they needed it to keep plantations running. This made them pull away from the North. Abraham Lincoln, the president at the time, feared there was no way to avoid civil war.

MEET JOHN

Imagine living during the Civil War. It had a great effect on kids' lives. For one kid named John, the effects of the Civil War hit close to home.

John lived on a farm in Kentucky, which was a slave state. His family owned slaves. Nat was a slave boy the same age as John. John and Nat played together when Nat didn't have to work.

John's father wanted to keep the country together. He joined the Union army. John's brother joined the Confederate army. He thought they would lose their slaves and farm if the Union won.

Many young boys lied about their age so they could join the army. They wanted to fight, just like their dads, uncles, and older brothers.

BOYS ON THE FRONT

Many young boys joined the armies as drummers. They played marching rhythms as armies marched into battle.

LITTLE FOOD

No one thought the war would last as long as it did. Most of the battles took place in the South. Farms near the battles were destroyed, and food became hard to find. The armies even took food from farms and used it to feed their **troops**. Many people—especially in the South—ran out of food as the war continued.

Farms such as the one pictured here fed many troops that passed through on their way to battle.

Union and Confederate troops took the food that once fed families.

John's farm in Kentucky was right in the middle of the fighting. When the Confederate and Union troops passed through, they took whatever food and supplies they needed. They left only potatoes and bread. That left John's family without much to eat.

MAKING DO

Troops took supplies, like clothing and blankets, from John's farm, too. John's mother didn't have enough cloth to make new clothes. She patched the holes in John and Nat's old clothes instead.

John and Nat dressed like other kids who lived during this time. Boys wore **knickers**, or short pants that gathered at the knee. **Suspenders** held up the knickers. The boys wore loose shirts, and they often went barefoot. Girls' clothing looked like the clothes their mothers wore. Slave children wore the same kinds of clothes as white children, but they usually weren't as nice.

The girls in this picture are wearing long skirts and tight-fitting tops. The boy is wearing clothes that look like his dad's uniform.

15

CIVIL WAR SCHOOLS

Kids during the Civil War went to school, but schools were different than they are now. Before the war started, John went to a one-room schoolhouse. He learned how to read, write, and do math.

Slaves weren't allowed to go to school. In the South, it was against the law for slaves to know how to read or write. John showed Nat what he learned in school, and Nat learned that way.

Many kids, including John, stopped going to school during the war. They had to work on the farms, since the men were off fighting.

This image shows what a school in New York looked like during the Civil War era. How is it different from schools of today?

SUPPORTING THE WAR AT SCHOOL

Some schools had children sing war songs before their morning lessons. It was their way of supporting the war and the soldiers who were away fighting.

LIFE DURING THE WAR

Living through the war was scary, especially since John's farm was so close to the fighting. John, Nat, and their families often hid in their cellar until the fighting stopped. They didn't want to get hurt.

On days when there was no fighting, John and Nat worked in the field. They also had chores to do. When they weren't working, they played outside or went fishing. John had a slingshot. He and Nat used it to hunt squirrels and rabbits. Any food they brought home could be cooked and eaten for dinner! This helped their families, especially when food supplies were low.

SLINGSHOT

WITNESSING THE WAR

Children who lived close to the fighting saw many scary parts of the war, such as battles, wounded soldiers, and more.

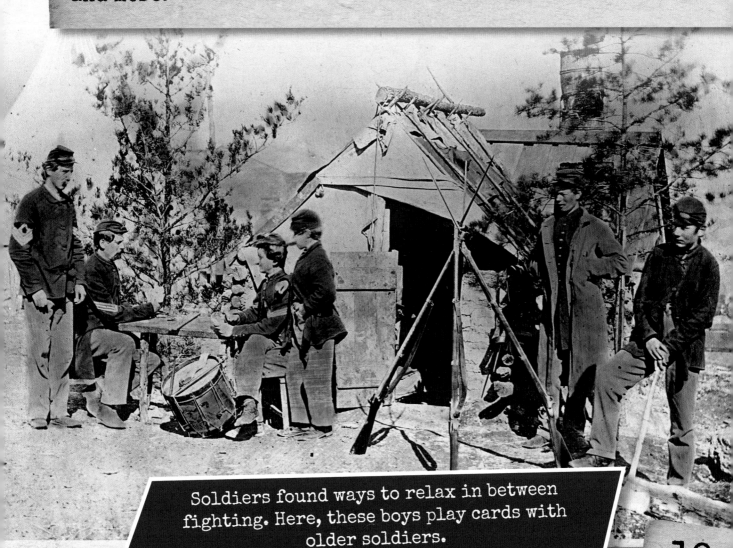

Soldiers found ways to relax in between fighting. Here, these boys play cards with older soldiers.

WORDS FROM THE FRONT

Families whose fathers, brothers, and sons went to war missed them very much. Soldiers wrote letters to their families. The letters told of the war and how the soldiers felt.

John's family checked for letters every day. When they arrived, John and his family read about the battles. They also read about how much the soldiers missed home.

Though they were on different sides, both John's father and brother wrote that many soldiers were sick or hurt. They also said there weren't enough doctors or supplies. Thousands of soldiers died because of this.

These soldiers may have been writing letters to their families about their time in the war. Letters let their families know they were safe.

A NATION UNITED

The Civil War ended in 1865. The North won, and the states were **united** again as one nation. The North's victory also ended slavery in the United States. With no education or money, former slaves had to find work and housing. Many moved north.

The Civil War destroyed the South. Buildings and farms were ruined, and many families became poor. Some Northerners traveled to help rebuild the South.

The Civil War changed the United States forever. But the **sacrifices** made by Americans like John and Nat helped the country become strong and united once again.

GLOSSARY

Confederacy: The group of 11 Southern states that separated from the United States in 1861.

era: A period of time.

knickers: Short pants that buttoned or gathered at the knee.

plantation: A large farm on which cotton, tobacco, rice, or sugarcane was grown.

sacrifice: Something given up for the sake of something more important.

slave: A person who is "owned" by another and forced to work for them.

suspenders: Straps worn over the shoulders to hold up pants.

troops: Soldiers or armed forces.

Union: The Northern states during the Civil War; also, a name for the United States as a whole.

united: Joined together.

INDEX

WEBSITES

Due to the changing nature of Internet links, PowerKids Press has developed
an online list of websites related to the subject of this book. This site is updated
regularly. Please use this link to access the list: www.powerkidslinks.com/hkl/civi